Prologue

Dear Soul is written in a way that tries to confront the ego and take the reader on a spiritual journey of thinking. The writing is confusing. The key things to remember is that I, Me, and My are representative of the ego. They represent our drive to win at everything. To have everything. We/Us/All on the other hand represents a more progressive united way of understanding life. It is about detachment. Living your life on trust, without out a plan. On a worthwhile pursuit of the divine. We/Us/All represents oneness. You and I are positive only in the case of the divine. Divine representing something greater. The concept of unity or oneness is essential to all faiths and science. I don't go into great detail about religious aspects, names, labels, practices. I do take from a variety of understandings and ideologies. Ultimately this is a whimsical formatted book of poetry that I want the reader to enjoy. I hope it gets the reader thinking, but if I had to choose, I would hope anyone that reads it, enjoys what they read.

- M.A.Q.I.B

Validation/Direction

I am like a little child
wandering about in a jungle
I go here, I go there
See a lion
It thinks to devour me
Before, it falls into a ditch
I clap and laugh
and think what a lovely beast
Then around the ditch
on my way
Dear Soul, you keep saving us
I perceive nothing

Another Tomorrow

Dear Soul,
there are too many tomorrows
between you and I
It has always been you and I
and an ocean
Then a raft made only of faith
Let us be together now
Dear Soul,
I grow thirsty

Surrounded by water
there is nothing here that
will quench my thirst
Sing to us Dear Soul
that I may sleep through
the tomorrows

You Bright Star

Dear Soul,
they are undeserving
You toil, round and round
we are warmed, loved
by your love
Born of your worship
or the worship of your
kindred
We see you Dear Soul
working diligently so that
we might be
We are with you in your
toil, in your service
We will learn, write, think,
experience for us all
Thank you, Dear Soul

Believers

We may never speak
but we know you
We love you
We see you and serve
you, Dear Soul
We will do what you ask
Be good and peace
Do not give up Dear Soul
Protect your intent
Protect it and forgive the rest
Yourself and everyone, everything
Dear Soul, we are united
Even though the ocean
separates you and I
Harbor no ill will, none

We'll Be Here

Dear Soul,
we'll be here
Keep me still
wanting, serving
Hold our mind in this
moment, so we may feel

its pleasure
Allow our imagination
out, let it go
Let it come and go
Dear Soul,
if it loves us
it will return
It'll recount stories
of its wander
Together again
until, Dear Soul,
keep still

Never Ending

Should we start from one
and never end
Whoa! If I try, I'd fail
So much gratitude
we have
And, still it is not enough
We are grateful
Also, full of shame, sorrow
I cannot repay
You will not accept
Spend time with us

Dear Soul, forgive my debt
We will give the rest to the
world in service
Love us Dear Soul
Fatten us with gratitude
Devour us Dear Soul

Earth

Dear Soul, they are not
grateful to you
Take our gratitude
and spread it out
We are here with you
You crafter of life
How diverse you
have made life
You are deserving
of service
But, they cut you down
Dear Soul, forgive us all
You are deserving
of gratitude
They do not know you
feel pain with every
sacrifice

We do Dear Soul
Take our gratitude and
forgive the others

They Make Love

That is not rain Dear Soul
You have made that up
Down it comes
Heavy, pounding, unrelenting
Dear Soul, the Earth
is not full, never
Dear Soul, then back up
Pulled back up again
by force
Again, but this time,
slow, beautiful, breezy,
a tickle
You call it a trickle
Dear Soul, it is not
raining
You perceive not, it
is love making
And, it is everywhere
Wonderfully done
Join in Dear Soul

Forget the illusion
for a moment
Join in

What Will You Play

Dear Soul, they love
their instruments
A beautiful melody
they do release
Just a painting
They love the showroom
To dress and look
at pictures
Just a song
Blind, are they to the
horizon
Deaf are they to the
string in us all
Ignorant of your skill,
Dear Soul
Use us lord, make
us a melody, Dear Soul
Let it sing in the hearts
of many
Dear Soul make us

into your score

Courage

We all have it,
true. We may not
keep it as you do
What you put in
the bedroom, another
puts in the attic
What one hides in
a locker, the other
places on a mantle
One in the dining
room
Dear Soul, one may
keep it under a pillow
What is in your study,
is what another wears
to work
Dear Soul, it is
a keepsake
If you do not see it,
it is hidden
with purpose

Scripture

One core truth
Yet if the wind manifested
and spoke, it would be lovely
If the ocean manifested,
it would be merciful
The stars would speak
of your burning compassion
The Earth would sing
of your judgement
Dear Soul, we shall
seek them out
Every leaf, every grain
of sand, every mountain
to hear about you
We will listen that we may
gather as the wind, shine
like the sun, create how
the Earth has done, and
flow as rivers do
That we might serve
you Dear Soul

Water and Wisdom

The water flows
The water falls
The water gives life
The water takes life
The water preserves life
The water travels and
carves mountains
The water is like
knowledge
And knowledge is like
water
No judgement, no river
No wisdom, no partition
No intelligence, no ocean
Judgement flows into
the ocean
And yet, intelligence never
touches the river
Give us wisdom,
Dear Soul
That we might guard
against anger, doubt,
and gratitude

Everything Is a Myth

Dear Soul, nothing is true

We will not, die
We will, live
There is no time
There is only you
There is no I, but
you and I are one
Religion hems me in
Science discovers only
what it divides
So enough is enough
We are going out
to play
Dear Soul,
come with us
I feel alone here
No one to play with
Dear Soul, we'll make
a game and play
with the wind,
will you watch

The How

I have never
seen the sun at the
Mosque

The clouds have not
come to church
Nor the grass
Nor the breeze
Nor the rivers
But they do
Surely, we know they do
Perfect in worship
We cannot capture
the how
So we go our way
Now, Dear Soul,
teach us how
this is true for
every person
That we might go
on our way

Silence

Don't lie and don't
be honest
Quiet now!
Swear by no one
and make no
oaths
Shush!!

Turn off the music,
so that the music
will play
Wait a moment
It is so much
more
Dear Soul, we feel
pleasure
Dear Soul, let
us stay

A Time and Some

Dear Soul, teach this
heart what to
think
Teach this mind
how to feel
Give a time, a time
and some
Let them understand
one another
This war has gone
on long enough
Let the pain
cease

Hide and Seek

Dear Soul, we have
found you out,
again
You don't seem
to understand the
game
You must go away
You must stay hidden,
out of sight
This time it was
the tic and the
toc
Dear Soul, next
time it'll be a
smell of a rose,
a thought, or a cry
Dear Soul, we will
find you
Everywhere, everywhere,
nowhere

Oh, Grateful Soul

Dear Soul, there was
a mountain in the sky

put there by you
All white, traveling through
all blue
It caught me in
thought
of some grateful thing
of some grateful way
Now it is gone
Replaced, the thought,
the cloud also
You put that there for
Us, Dear Soul
How descriptive you are
So forgive it, let us
move on
What is next
our dear love

Surrender

A doctor is useless
at the battle
until it ends
The bodies are collected
The dead for the grave
The sick, the wounded
for treatment

Now the doctor is valuable
Dear Soul, there is no
help while you are
fighting
The doctor does not seek
patients, save for profit
They are brought in to
be saved
Dear Soul, everyone
you send, shine your
light through us
Your love, Our love
Dear Soul, we will
only seek your face
That we may profit

Fly With Us, In Us

Dear Soul every bit of
love you will ever
need, you have
Seek nothing
Desire nothing
Give away greed
Give away the world
Give away doubt
Let go of attachment

Undo yourself
Do not weigh down
this soul
Let go Dear Soul
Now fly
Come, come Dear Soul
If you cannot fly
then you do not understand
Again, enough love you have
A full provision given
Do not thirst
Do not hunger
Do not envy
Do not lust
Do not encourage
Do not support
You are not in control
Dear Soul, let go
Now fly
If you cannot fly then
you lack mercy
Come, come Dear Soul
Move in, become one, align
Do not judge, don't reason
withhold punishment
Run from fear
Cease understanding

There! There we go Dear Soul
Be as light and fly away

The Master

I, will not!
Dear Soul, say to you,
give me this and
take me there
We will say master,
what is next
We await your surprise
Tell us of your plans to
heal this heart
Tell us of your plans to
subdue our ego
Tell us of your plans to
take away our burden
Your plans to give us
wealth, as you see it
We will not tell you,
Dear Soul
We will await your voice
Sound judgement for all

Abandonment

Don't run after what
hasn't been given to you
Don't argue, there is
no reason to
Give up your plans
They are not
yours to make
Undue your goals
Let them free
Loosen your belt
Align Dear Soul, you are
with us now
We will take care of you
No need for ambition
You will eat
No need for hunger
You will drink
No need for thirst
There will be love
No need for desire
This soul shall be estranged
from the world

The Market

Dear Soul, they love

the market
To buy, to sell,
to be seen
Dear Soul, they love
the water but hate
the well
They purchase what is
otherwise free
The tables have been turned
back up right again
The seller loves the profit
The buyer loves the fruit
The seller never says where
they came upon it
The buyer never asks
Dear Soul,
it must grow somewhere
Take us to the tree
Dear Soul, bring us
to the well
There is no need for
the marketplace

Record Keeper

Dear Soul, lord,
you are there keeping a tally

Recording our speech
Recording our intent
Recording our ways
So, you must do this
Dear Soul, you must keep record
We are grateful to you dear
Love, record it please
We are grateful for your
presence, record it please
We are grateful for your
integrity, record it please
We are grateful for your
indifference, record it please
We are grateful for your
humility, record it please
You do know of my failures, my
missteps, my deliberations
Forgive, record it please
Forgive all, blot it out
Let it vanish, record it please
Let harmony rule over chaos
And mercy reign in judgement
Record it please
Last night as we walked, there
was a halo over the moon
Wider than normal, all the colors
of the rainbow

The clouds made it more
beautiful even
Record it please
That we were grateful for
that sight, Dear Soul
And, for your company and service

Come, Live

Dear Soul, give up food
and what lives inside you
will die

Dear Soul, give up water and
you and your physical
will die

Dear Soul, feed the life
that dwells inside you and
the plants and animals
will die

Dear Soul, give up death
so that all may
live

Imagination

Come out Dear Soul
I am, a bit weary
We, go work, and I
go rest
We earn and I will sleep
for a while
Let me switch and let them
see us
Let I hide and be no more
They hate my sight, they
will love us
We sing and dance
We go through walls, fly
through skies and heavens
We are much kinder
We are a sweet note
Make work as play Dear Soul
If we become weary, I
will return
So be strong in your play,
Dear Soul
And, we will stay out,
all the while

The Lion

Oh, I am like a lion
They say, Dear Soul
I hunt and take what
is mine
I am a killer
I am strong
I am ferocious and to be
feared
I, I, I!
Cover them Dear Soul
Give them what they desire
The lion is meek and
eats only it's fill
The lion has not cut
down any tree
The lion hunts the gazelle
which frees the grass to grow
Now the gazelle may eat
The lion eats no plant and
does not extend its territory
The lion is ferocious for the
sake of righteousness
The lion is feared for the
sake of harmony
The lion kills so that it may

maintain its strength
Cover them Dear Soul
Give them what they desire
Let the lion rule and
harmony reign

Put More

Dear Soul, how much hope
does one need
We put out the body
The brain is good and have
given of your goodness
Put more
Give this soul hope
Enough hope for a lifetime
Dear Soul, put more
Give this soul hope
Enough hope for two lifetimes
Dear Soul, put more
Give this soul hope
Enough hope for ten lifetimes
Dear Soul, put more
Never stop
Light is, hope, to carry
Useful and enduring
Put more

The Voice

That is not the wind Dear Soul
But, a command, come to life
Gather, Dear Soul
The clouds come running
Even to call them clouds is
to be a fool
Those are not clouds, Dear Soul
It is grace
Look how easily they bring
about the rain
No, not rain but love and
sustenance
And it pours out onto the
Earth and it is not full
Truth rather, the Earth is truth
Judgement awaits in soil
Awaits in the rivers
Awaits in the trees
Dear Soul, this, where we
pick the fruit
Where we harvest the crop
A mercy you have harvested
Dear Soul, the result of a
single command

Stop making decisions
Await the voice
Await the command
Dance with love from assignment
to assignment
Until this soul has become a
mercy taken from truth
Sweet fruit for all
to enter joy

Angels, Love, and Mercy

You have not lost
There is time Dear Soul
You have slept a while
And we have not left you
Dear Soul, when the fatigue
wears off we will be
present
We can start anew and the
rest was a dream
Do not think of a dream
as a prison
Do not judge your soul
that is not possible
Take our hand Dear Soul
Walk with us

We will rehearse of heaven,
angels, love, mercy and
no more
Forget the dream
Wake up
Love awaits Dear Soul
Love

We Are the Light

Dear Soul, we have never
been to this place
I do not know these
streets and perceive no sun
There is warmth, no sun
Dear Soul, there is mercy
and no sky
There is no direction, but
there is guidance
I am cold
Forgive my fear, Dear Soul
I am just a child
Yours, my love
Still I am shuttering at
my ignorance
Forgive, and forgive, and forgive
I may fall in somewhere

It is dark, it is so dark
I cannot perceive any light
Dear Soul, take our hand
Lead us through this new
place until we are one

The Roadside

I am not your prisoner
Still, I cannot escape you
Far from righteousness, Dear Soul
I have thought up every sin,
every sin
But the hands did not move
and the feet do not flee
You will forgive it or to
hell, or around again
Dear Soul, I have not gone
up to the mountain
Dear Soul, I have no ministry
I have not preached or
poached from the devil
So ordinary am I, Dear Soul
Still, you found me out
There is no power except
what you share
No words that I can use

to motivate
Easy for you to leave
me at the roadside
Adrift, wandering, a fool
You stay with me and
accompany me place to place
Teach me gratitude
So that sin will be no more
So that we may exist

Smile

Dear Soul, within me
is a devil, an ingrate
A believing fool tries
to put distance between us
Dear Soul, frustrate him
If he beats me today
return us to you right after
Forgive us like nothing
has occurred
Like only you may
I think to forgive as
you and fall forward
into judgement
Teach us, Dear Soul
not to think

Forgive for us as you may
Teach us to smile instead
That is easier

They Will Not

The world does not want
help, Dear Soul
They love this place
They think nothing of
their share
They praise the prison
because it is all they know
We come calling to them,
Dear Soul
"Look outside the walls"
They will not
"Walk with us out of
this palace. It is
not guarded"
They will not
They have made a bed
for the prison
A couch and art
"Come out", we scream!
Dear Soul, they will not
They hate us for trying

We cannot hold up here,
Dear Soul
But from outside the wall
In the garden
We will call to them
Forever, Dear Soul
We will

Oh Adam

Dear Soul, the world
tries to capture you
To lock you away
in some rigid ideology
Some false concept
They say I have him
contained here, come worship
But, here you are with us
There you are in the soil
Again, in the beast
Dear Soul, they try to
paint your figure
They fool themselves and
so many others
There prophet is profit
They play the same game
in different arenas

They swear one is above
the other
This is no sport
Dear Soul, we will worship
you
Dear Soul, in the soil
Dear Soul, in the beast
Dear Soul, in the arena
Wherever you may be,
we will find you
and prostrate our soul

The Kingdom

Dear Soul, they ran in
found a room, barricaded
the door and hid
One yelled out, "all of you
hide, let no one in"
We called to them
"Dear Soul, you are home,
do not hide"
Dear Soul, another group
ran in, paused, saw us
They did the same
One called out "this room
is the holy one. What you

Desire is within"
We called to them
"Dear Soul, there is no
room, you are home"
Then another, and another,
another Dear Soul
We called out, "you are home"
some come out, but just
a few, Dear Soul
We called to them, "Dear
Soul, what brought you out?"
They responded, "we never
Left, dear lord"
So we responded, "you are
home, move about"

Pour Out

Sweet, Sweet, Sweet,
Dear Soul
Is the joy of this heart
The heart is under your
protection and bears
your mark
Unlock the door to
this soul
Hide this pleasure no more

Break it if you must
But, let the light out
and create a tilt
Let it pour out as
Waterfalls
Let it be relentless and
enjoyed by all who are
near and far
Unlock the door, Dear Soul
Protect us but do not
guard against outsiders
anymore
It is well now, time has
come
They have no defense

The Olive Tree

Ah, live, ah
Dear Soul, we have eaten
of the tree and tasted of
its beauty
How sweet the tree,
Dear Soul
You are still sweeter
Beauty, peace, prosperity,
Dear Soul

Ah, love, ah
Dear Soul, you did hide
its presence from us
while we took of its
shade
Dear Soul, its oil was
hidden while we tasted of
its sustenance
Dear Soul, teach us to play
as you do
Teach us to hide our
works in the light
Take us away from the
world, banish us, but
let them see our work
Dear Soul, your sweetness
is like shade and your shade
is like fruit
Continue Dear Soul,
through us we will
carry the branch and
fly away to and fro, working
Ah, peace, ah

Abundance

Chaos, chaos rules,

Dear Soul
Harmony awaits to enter
Chaos loves chaos
and seeks harmony
no more
So, the fire burns
and it grows, Dear Soul
Harmony awaits, it will
not beat the door down
Harmony awaits, it will
not put out the fire
The fire is the
abundance
Let it burn and
let it build
Harmony, "we are amongst
the blaze. When will
you enter?"
"When it roars open for
us, calling out for
Stability"
Dear Soul, until, wait
with patience and glee
Stare out at harmony and
become one
Chaos cannot refuse
the harmonious soul

Taste of the abundance

The Handhold

I am insecure and
lacking in power
I am egotistical and ugly
I am full of shame
and regret
I am a sinner
I am weak, dumb, blind,
and directionless
Leave, me!
Dear Soul, when the
children are young they
dress and play as the adults
Dear Soul, when the
children are old they
dress and play as the adults
Take our hand Dear Soul
and undress us
We are powerful and
safe
We are limitless with beauty
and limitless indeed
We are the guiltless
Hidden from shame

We abhor evil and we
are the light of life
We, Dear Soul, we lord
We forever and forever

Some Say

Dear Soul, you see
the wayfarer and make
no deposit
No deposit into your
own bank
Some say they have
made a choice
Some say they are lazy
and will not work
Some say, some say,
some say
Some will not even smile
Oh heart of ours, we
give you permission, grieve
Grieve, Dear Soul, until
you are cured of misery
Dear Soul when the grief
passes, die
Die, and die, and die
Until you are cured of

misery
Glory is the lord that
shines the light and
brings the dead to life
Dear Soul when you have
been born once again,
seek compassion
Dear Soul if you cannot find
the tree, then go
to the market
If you cannot pay,
then beg
Dear Soul, beg, and beg,
and beg again
Dear Soul, then eat
what is given
Until you are full and
cured of misery
We await your return

To Hell With I

Dear Soul, throw I into
the fire and let it burn
Dear Soul, put me in hell
and lock the door
Leave Dear Soul

For an eternity
Let it be a lesson to
the faithful, the grateful
We know, Dear Soul
It is our time
Give us life and love
from your share
A new heart and a new
spirit Dear Soul
Let us breath for the
first time
Let us walk and dance
for the first time
Let us also see how
wonderful it is for the
first time
Dear Soul, you have no
pleasure in death
Turn us and we shall live
as you have ordered
Dear Soul, if you will,
we will
So, we will make gratitude our
religion
We will make the infinite
surrender our way
Love, love, love, surrounds

us now

Sand on My Feet

Dear Soul, this night
we did travel
It must have been some
glorious place
We must have played
and played
Dear Soul, I still cannot
see in the dark
I am blind to the diversity
and power of the spirit
But, Dear Soul,
we did travel
And, we did play
We do not need to see
where we are
Blind is love
We awoke grateful and
in joy
In joy Dear Soul
I, does not like the
beach, Dear Soul
But, we love the water
and the sand

The rhythm, the color,
the peace
Also, Dear Soul,
your company
We will go anywhere
with you
So, affix love to our
soul and let no one
separate us
Let us walk

Law of Attraction

Dear Soul, may tomorrow
never come
Let us ascend today
No prep, no plan, no goal,
no understanding,
no judgement, no regret
Dear Soul let us join
your network
Introduce us to the
holy ones
Let us see the faces
of the ones that save us
Let us smile at there
selflessness

Give us there will
to serve
I cannot see any profound
way to attract some life
unknown
You know, it is in your book
The book is sealed with
you in joy
We will Dear Soul, is the only
way that presents itself
No judgement, no prayer, no ask
I cannot reconcile trust
and asking
We will ask for trust
I cannot reconcile worship
and prayer
We will worship through prayer
I cannot reconcile judgement
and mercy
We will make mercy our judgement
Dear Soul understanding is yours
We will be grateful

Perception

Dear Soul, how sweet
is the fruit that you refuse

On and on about an
unfair world
Down into the grave
You are not spent
I, wants out and yet
it digs deeper
The lord of hosts forgives
Back again Dear Soul
You are hungry
Sweet is the fruit
we put on the tree
that you pass by
on your way to
the market
Oh soul, you go without
money and put
it to credit
Woe, woe Dear Soul
I, has not paid
back the debt
and continues to buy
The lord of hosts forgives
Back again Dear Soul
Poor are they so, I,
refuses the spouse
Dear Soul, the lord loves them
They cannot be the one

And I, cannot be alone
I, gives their power and
abundance to the wealthy
I, is left without
The lord of host forgives
"How many times Dear Soul?"
"As long as they turn back
we will forgive."
Back again, Dear Soul

Blessed Are The

This place, Dear Soul
It is not like home
Here they say the wealthy
are humble and the
humble are poor
Here the poor are not
meek, but arrogant
and ambitiously so
Here the male has become
female and the female
has become male
They are still not whole
Dear Soul, they just
change attire
You wear this and I

will wear that
Here there is no moment
for rest
Dear Soul, they
sport in the Mosque, the
Church, the Synagogue,
and every holy place
Zeus has been replaced
Athena has been replaced
Odin, Ra, Set, and
Venus have all been
Replaced
Every Idol
The worshippers are more
fervent than ever
And every rich and talented
one is called up to
Olympus
Dear Soul, the meek survive
We see them about, holy
and good
Filled with The Spirit
So, Dear Soul, all is well
We are with them,
tending to the crop

The Warrior

Dear Soul, we will
take you to see the
warrior
When in battle the
warrior fought vigorously
When the odds were not
in their favor they
called on us
They answered every call
and slew the ones we
ordered away
We did come upon them
They were jolly and full
of happiness
They ran with the children
and pet animals
We have never seen
anyone so joyful
"Where is the warrior", we
asked?
"There, there they are"
They are so wonderful
They are so subdued
That cannot be a warrior
Dear Soul, they were at war
Now they are with us

Their sorrow is now happiness
Their pain is now contentment
The wounds stitched, the heart
healed, and their sins
forgiven
They took no enemy from
their enemy
They mourned every soul
that took their sword
We replaced their sword
with sobriety, love,
giving, and service
Dear Soul when you return,
tell them how to be
Do not bring the war home
Do not fight after the battle
After they surrender,
you surrender

Oneness

A crab, a cup, a tiger,
a whale
Dear Soul, all are one
A sailboat, Jupiter, a rodent,
the birds
Dear Soul, we are all one

Orion opens up for Aquarius
And she calls for
her moment
Sand from the moon comes
from her teacup and
spreads out
The constellations pray
for unity
They signal for peace
The bear at her back,
The elephant at one side
At the other, eight legs
traveling on a beast
that travels on Saturn
Oneness they call out
Dear Soul, teach this soul
to listen
Here come the monks
They sit and they wait
Open our ears and let
them see
Open our eyes and let
them hear
A smell, a thought, we feel
A touch, a taste, we feel
Dear Soul, dear light, dear
lord, you are a

wonderful host
Free the peasants that
they may become slaves
Crowned by your glory
Your light, your love
All while you watch

Signs

Dear Soul see us when
we pass by
Dear Soul see the birds
we send you
Dear Soul listen as they
preach
Hear our voice and quite
the noise
There is no matter that
cannot be resolved
No matter at all
The understanding of the
world is but that of
some art
Dear Soul, see us in
song and dance
No matter
See us in play and

sport
No matter
See us in talent
and games
No matter
See us in women and men
No matter
The tree, the cloud, stars,
planets, all must come
down for worship, prostate
See Dear Soul, we are
not alone
We are all one
No matter at, all

Blemished

We do not make love
for selfish reasons
No Dear Soul
Service is the call, so
come out
The one who loves to
serve is a virgin
before the lord
Touched, Blemished, like
nothing you have seen

Dear Soul, serve
Serve and we will dress
this soul in all white
and lead this soul through
dirt and filth
Blemished
Begin a virgin in all white
Now live always the same
Blemished
What touches, Dear Soul,
will fall off, forgiveness
blemished
So, walk with us, dance with
us, rehearse with us,
as we serve

Everything, All

Dear Soul, everything has
a soul
I cannot perceive my own
so I cannot perceive
the others
Perceive the light inside
that extends out
It covers a multitude
of things

Yes, the cow has its soul
Yes, the bird has its soul
Yes, the sheep have their soul
But, Dear Soul that is not
all that is not everything
Dear Soul, the tree, yes
Dear Soul, the plant, yes
Dear Soul, the ocean, yes
But that is not all that is
not everything
Dear Soul, the Earth, yes
Dear Soul, the star, yes
Dear Soul, the universe, yes
But that is not all that
is not everything
Perceive, Dear Soul,
Perceive

The Falcon

Dear Soul as we sat
you stared
High up in the tree
you took notice
I cannot understand your
query, your position
I cannot know what you

thought or what you gave
I do not know why you come
or why you stared
We did stare back,
Dear Soul
I dare not hold your gaze
Oh, bird of prey
you did bring the sun
up in Egypt
Dear Soul, you do rule
over all the birds
Guard us Dear Soul and
share a vision of wisdom
We will follow you, Dear
Soul, to meaning and purpose
Dear Soul, find us work
of service, pleasing to
the lord

Be, Come

Dear Soul, the whole world
awaits your entry
So, come out in cups
spread across the table
of life
Let them run in from

all over
Let them drink this
soul and let it
refill without pouring
The world awaits, the
world is full of thirst
They must be emptied
So, they can be filled
again
By, The Spirit alone
Dear Soul, they live in
fatigue, lay on misery,
wear ingratitude,
and eat of pain
Offered humility they will
not partake
Pride they ask for
and pour me contempt
Yet they seek love
So, come out Dear Soul
Let them feel us
Be all consuming
Forget reason this day
Everyday

100 Ways to Love

So, few are the ways
to hate
Yet the roads are full
and traffic frustrates
Jealousy tempts, cruelty
erodes, envy scorns
Oh soul, Dear Soul
Malice demeans, vengeance
is a foe, resentment is the oppressor
Oh soul, Dear Soul
The liar is treacherous, bitterness
flatters your thoughts, and
injustice is a bastard
Oh soul, Dear Soul
This is but one road,
a clutter, the road
of desire
Leading to misery
Dear Soul, a hundred
ways to love
A hundred roads
Fly, run, walk, crawl, the
streets are clear and some
will help us along the way
So, Dear Soul, take care,
be kind, and travel
patiently

Trust that heaven awaits

Read

Dear Soul, the readers read
and their eyes gaze down
Dear Soul, we'll read also,
but keep our gaze upward
Now read Dear Soul
For the words are alive
and they are everywhere
Everywhere is a story
Everywhere is a kindness
Everywhere is love
Everywhere is a romance
with a lovely ending
Everywhere is a tale of
great mystery
Everywhere is a drama
with a wonderful twist
See us Dear Soul as
you gaze up at the stars
We will play music as
they dance
Keep us in mind until
the adventures end
The fantasy is heavenly

So, bow Dear Soul, bow
Do not wait for the
curtain call
Bow Dear Soul, bow

The Unseen

Dear Soul, love at a distance
Be as the starlight
Do not chase after service
Be unseen and all will
be presented to you
Be Dear Soul, grow and
be beautiful and they will
find you out
The mountain does not
call out
No one says you are
to rigid, oh mountain
But from the world
over they come to see,
to love, to study
Now us Dear Soul
We are greater than
the mountain
Deeper than the seas
So, believe and be

as lightning Dear Soul
Be as a cool storm in
the desert Dear Soul
Be!
Better, the wind, Dear Soul,
which no one sees and
no one knows
May they only feel us
Hover, Dear Soul
Shine, Dear Soul
Bless, Dear Soul
Love, Dear Soul
We have permission
We are the vicegerent of
the merciful benefactor
So, deal

Reject Me

Oh soul, Dear Soul
They continue to reject me
They will not stop hating me
I am so despised and
rejected
I could not feel worse
Away with me, hide me
Dear Soul

Put me in some foreign
universe
Locked in an unknown
dimension
Put me at the core
of a dying star
Let that star die
Away with time, away
with me
Still Dear Soul, find a door
and close it behind
Lock the door
Take the key and give
it to a young star,
far away
Let it burn
Never to be seen after
We know, Dear Soul
We shall endure
Enough with I
Enough with me
Enough with my
We, now, Dear Soul
We shall endure

Give Direction

Dear Soul, I was born
in the house of the
merchant
I was taught and treated well
There was love
And discipline
Then the lord put me out
I could not return
So off we went hand in
hand with the merchant
Suddenly there was a light
Fearlessly we went in,
until we became the light
Then there were three
a man, a woman, a child
The light originated with the
shepherd and was more
glorious than the sun
Brighter, warmer, more loving
They looked over the sheep
The sheep like dots filling
the Earth over
The merchant took our hand
and we left
I did not want to leave
Then there was the king
The ruler of judgement

and wealth
Dear Soul, sing for us
the merchant spoke
It is my friend
We will sing
All together lovely was the
voice of wisdom
His father played music in
union with dance
All at once
As the father moved, he
was as a star with
six ends
We were with gratitude
Gratitude played music
and harmony danced
while wisdom sang
Then the merchant took
our hand and we left
I did not want to leave
We came to two
mountains, one greater
than the other
They held in place
all the Earth
Then they were like men
This is our brother and

this is our father
Nine stars gazed down
upon them
Peace, love, affection,
service was all we could
feel
I did not want to leave
But, then they let us by
and the merchant brought
me to the ocean
No raft, Dear Soul, I cannot
Be! We persisted, walking
across the water with ease
There was a monk, under
a tree and he seemed
to be asleep
He was perfectly aligned
He spoke twelve kind
words and that was all
We sat, closed our eyes
And became one
When the eye opened
We were home
And there they all were
The merchant, the shepherd,
The king and his father, the
mountains, and the monk

And others living inside of them
They were always there
but I could not perceive
Seven as one Dear Soul
Undivided sharing your
love with all
Dear Soul, that was the
way I took to we

One Gives, One Receives

Dear Soul, remember we
are all one
So be whole and give
And then Dear Soul be
grateful
So be whole and receive
And then Dear Soul be
grateful
Dear Soul give, and
give, and give
Then leave and expect
nothing in return
Dear Soul, let the light in
Be full of gratitude and
allow some more
We have begun to plan

The same day we pressed
down the universe and
expanded its soul
We knew of what we
would give through
this soul
We have planned a
surprise, Dear Soul
Pressed down will it
return, expanding out
upon this soul
Receive, and receive,
and receive
And remember we are one
Now give, and give,
and give
Dear Soul, this is
the game
There is no gender,
no orientation, and
no matter
Lay off seriousness and
come play
It is a wonderful game